Presents

UKULELE
A COMPLETE COURSE

**Written & Method By
John McCarthy**

Adapted By: Jimmy Rutkowski
Supervising Editor: John McCarthy
Music Transcribing & Engraving: Jimmy Rutkowski
Production Manager: John McCarthy
Layout, Graphics & Design: Jimmy Rutkowski
Photography: Jimmy Rutkowski
Copy Editor: Cathy McCarthy

Cover Art Direction & Design:
Jimmy Rutkowski

HL142174
ISBN: 978-1-4950-1145-0
Second Edition
Produced by John McCarthy

T0066248

Table of Contents

Digital eBook

When you register this product at the lesson support site RockHouseMethod.com, you will receive a digital version of this book. This interactive eBook can be used on all devices that support Adobe PDF. This will allow you to access your book using the latest portable technology any time you want.

Words From the Author

Playing ukulele is a rewarding art form that will last you a lifetime, I discovered that fact shortly after I was given my first ukulele. I have spent my career sharing the passion I have for ukulele with others. With my ukulele method, I truly believe you too will enjoy years of fun and will pass on the passion you discover. If you follow the method step-by step you will be successful and enjoy playing ukulele for years to come. When I designed The Rock House® Method, my mission was to create the most complete and fun way to learn. I accomplished this by developing and systematically arranging a modern method based on the needs and social demands of today's players. I not only tell you where to put your fingers, I show you ways to use what you learn so that you can make music right from the start. I know it is hard to imagine, but even the all-time greats started somewhere, there was a time when they too didn't even know what a chord was. As you progress as a ukulele player, keep your mind open to all styles of music. Set-up a practice schedule that you can manage, be consistent, challenge yourself and realize everyone learns at a different rate. Be patient, persistent and remember music is supposed to be fun!

NOW, GET EXCITED, this is it. YOU are going to play ukulele!

The Rock House® Method Learning System

This learning system can be used on your own or guided by a teacher. Be sure to register for your free lesson support at RockHouseMethod.com. Your member number can be found inside the cover of this book.

Lesson Support Site: Once registered, you can use this fully interactive site along with your product to enhance your learning experience, expand your knowledge, link with instructors, and connect with a community of people around the world who are learning to play music using The Rock House® Method.

Bonus Video Lessons: Once you have registered using your member number located on the last page of this book you can access additional lesson videos to take your ukulele playing to the next level!

Quizzes: Each level of the curriculum contains multiple quizzes to gauge your progress. When you see a quiz icon go to the *Lesson Support* site and take the quiz. It will be graded and emailed to you for review.

Audio Examples & Play Along Tracks: Demonstrations of how each lesson should sound and full band backing tracks to play certain lessons over.

Icon Key

These tell you there is additional information and learning utilities available at RockHouseMethod.com to support that lesson.

Backing Track

Backing track icons are placed on lessons where there is an audio demonstration to let you hear what that lesson should sound like or a backing track to play the lesson over. Use these audio tracks to guide you through the lessons. **Use your member number to register at the *Lesson Support* site and download the corresponding audio tracks.**

Metronome

Metronome icons are placed next to the examples that we recommend you practice using a metronome. You can download a free, adjustable metronome on the *Lesson Support* site.

Worksheet

Worksheets are a great tool to help you thoroughly learn and understand music. These worksheets can be downloaded at the *Lesson Support* site.

Tuner

You can download the free online tuner on the *Lesson Support* site to help tune your instrument.

History of the Ukulele

In 1879, the Portuguese master craftsman and instrument maker Manuel Nunes arrived in the Hawaiian Islands with Joao Fernandes and Augustine Dias. They were immigrants who came to work in the sugar cane fields. Together they invented and developed the ukulele taking basic designs of instruments from their native home.

Hawaiians were not only impressed with the beautiful sounds these instruments could make, but also with the speed these musicians' fingers flew on the fingerboard. It is said, they in turn began calling this instrument the Ukulele, which roughly translates as "Jumping Fleas". The ukulele became Hawaii's most popular musical instrument. All who learned the art of the ukulele loved it, from fisherman and farmers to Kings and Queens.

It was around 1915 that the ukulele's popularity migrated to mainland United States. A Hawaiian music craze had hit starting in San Francisco and made its way across the country causing ukulele sales to soar. The craze even swept across the ocean to Europe and Asia.

The great demand for ukuleles in turn lead to a demand for ukulele manufacturing. Of the three original Portuguese ukulele makers, only Manuel Nunes remained and by 1910, orders were so numerous that he could not keep up with the demand. New competitors entered the field sometimes bringing unique design differences, tonal qualities and innovations.

Competition took a new turn as mainland guitar manufacturers entered the ukulele market around 1915. In the 1920's, mainland manufacturers such as Gibson, Harmony, Regal, National, Dobro and Martin were mass-producing ukuleles by the thousands. Martin produced their first ukulele in 1916 based on the Nunes design.

The ukulele has become popular with young and old. It is light, portable and with a little practice, fairly easy to strum a simple song. Its happy tone is almost infectious and can easily bring a smile to any face.

Types of Ukuleles

Ukuleles come in different sizes and models. The soprano is the most common and smallest giving it a high pitched tone. Here are the four most common model:

• **Soprano** – This is the standard ukulele. The soprano is the ukulele that is most easily recognized because it is the tiniest and the tone is typically the one associated with ukuleles. The soprano ukulele is the one often given to novices who are interested in learning the ukulele.

• **Concert** – This one is also referred to as the alto ukulele. It is slightly larger than the soprano model, and it has a 15" scale neck compared to 13" on the soprano. This makes it a better choice for people with larger hands. It has a fuller tone, which may or may not appeal to you.

• **Tenor** – This type of ukulele can come with different numbers of strings, there are 4 and 6 string models. It is larger and has a fuller tone than the concert ukulele.

• **Baritone** – This is the largest of the ukuleles and resembles a mini-guitar. It can even be tuned like a guitar. It has the deepest tone and is usually the most expensive model.

Parts of the Ukulele

It's important to know the parts of the ukulele so you can follow the program effectively. All ukuleles are made up of three main sections: the body, the neck and the headstock.

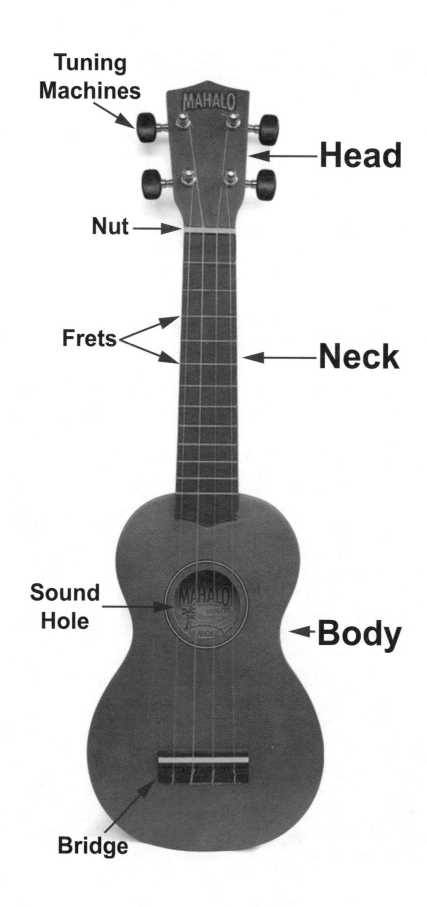

Names of the Open Strings & Tuning

On your ukulele the strings are named 1st – A, 2nd – E, 3rd – C, 4th – G. A great way to remember the open strings is to use an acronym creating a word for each letter name. The following is a silly acronym I created: **A**n – **E**lf – **C**an't - **G**row. Try to create your own saying to help you memorize the names of the open strings.

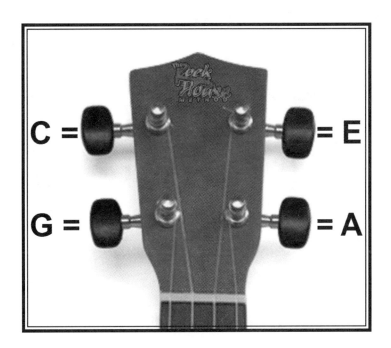

Holding the Ukulele

Your left hand should curl in a C shape with your thumb planted in the middle of the back of the neck. Your fingertips will be used to fret notes.

Finger Numbers

As you progress through this book I will be referencing your fretting hand fingers with numbers. Memorize these now so you can follow along with ease.

Left hand or fretting hand:

Index Finger = 1

Middle Finger = 2

Ring Finger = 3

Pinky Finger = 4

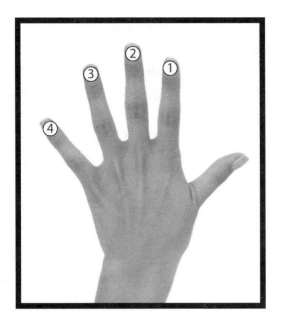

Reading Tablature

Tablature (or tab) is a number system for reading notes on the ukulele. It does not require you to have knowledge of standard music notation.

The four lines of the tablature staff represent each of the four strings. The top line is the 1st string. The bottom line is the 4th string. The numbers placed directly on these lines are the fret number to play each note. Underneath the staff is a series of numbers. These numbers tell you which left hand finger to fret the notes with.

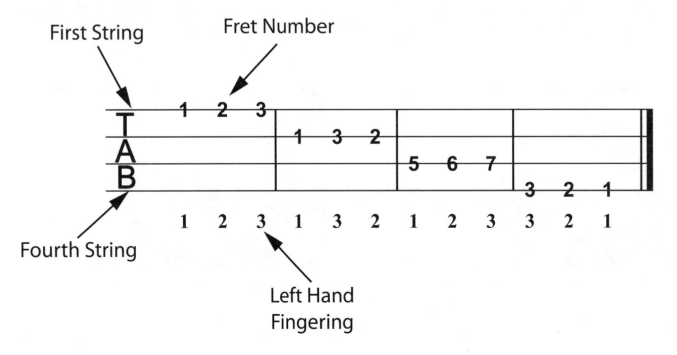

First String

Fret Number

Fourth String

Left Hand Fingering

10

Picking Techniques

There are two options for picking the ukulele. You can use a hard felt pick placed between your thumb and index fingers or you can use your fingers. When using your fingers the thumb and index fingers are commonly used.

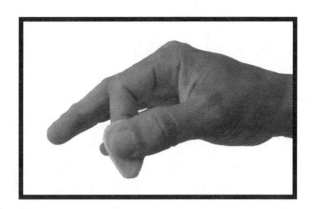

Picking Exercises

Here's a few alternate picking exercises to help coordinate your right hand. The following symbols indicate whether a note is picked in an up or a down direction:

⊓ - **downpick (pick down toward the floor)**

∨ - **uppick (pick up toward the ceiling)**

Exercise 1

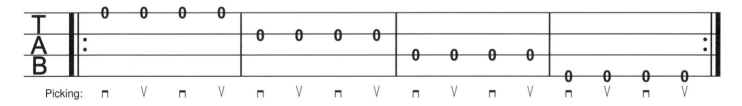

Exercise 2

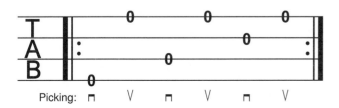

Finger Exercises

This is a finger exercise in tablature that will build coordination and strengthen your fingers. It's designed to help stretch your hand out, so keep your fingers spread across the first three frets, one finger per fret. Leave your first finger anchored in place and reach for the following three notes by stretching your hand out.

With your right hand, use alternate picking in a consistent down-up-down-up pendulum motion. Alternate picking will help develop speed, smoothness and technique. Practice this exercise using the metronome for timing and control.

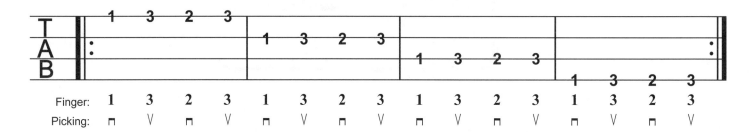

| Finger: | 1 | 3 | 2 | 3 | 1 | 3 | 2 | 3 | 1 | 3 | 2 | 3 | 1 | 3 | 2 | 3 |
| Picking: | ⊓ | V | ⊓ | V | ⊓ | V | ⊓ | V | ⊓ | V | ⊓ | V | ⊓ | V | ⊓ | V |

Reading Chord Charts

A chord is a group of notes played together. A chord chart (chord diagram) is a graphic representation of part of the fretboard (as if you stood the ukulele up from floor to ceiling and looked directly at the front of the neck). The vertical lines represent the strings; the horizontal lines represent the frets. Chord diagrams show which notes to play and which strings they are played on. The black dots within the graph represent fretted notes and show you where your fingers should go.

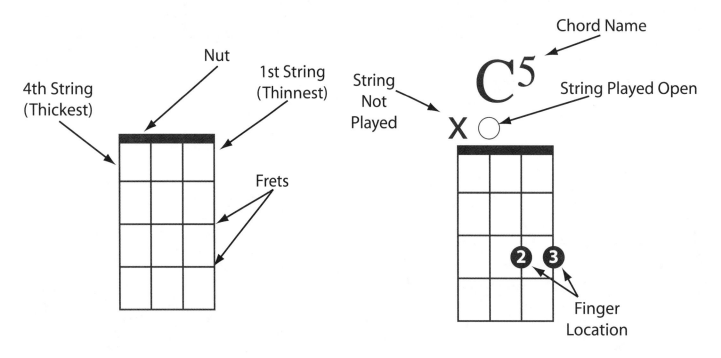

Your First Chords

Read the following chord charts to play your first chords. Pick each one note at a time then strum it down with one swift motion across the strings.

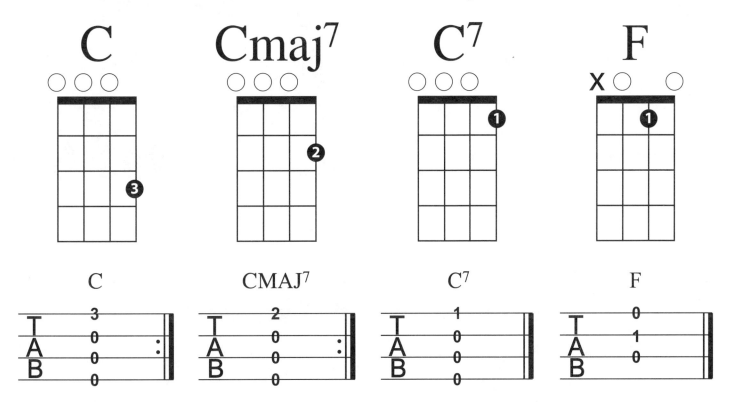

Strum Techniques

A common strumming technique uses the thumb and index fingers. Using the pad of each finger strum down with the thumb and up with the index finger in a loose relaxed motion.

You can also use the felt pick to strum chords holding the pick between your thumb and index fingers and pivot your arm from your elbow in a down up motion. Make sure to keep the motion small, not going too far past the strings in either motion.

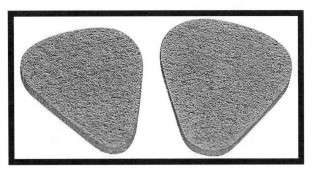

Felt Picks

Reading Strum Patterns

Throughout this book you will see diagrams showing you the strum pattern to use for the exercise. The arrows show which way to strum, and the letters below the arrows show you to use either your thumb (T) and first finger (I) or if you are using a pick, downstroke (D) and upstroke (U).

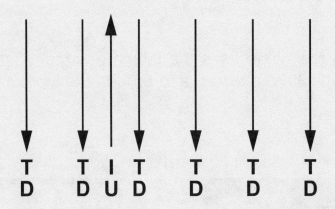

The Rhythm Staff

The rhythm staff will be used in this book to show song rhythms. Memorize the parts on the staff below.

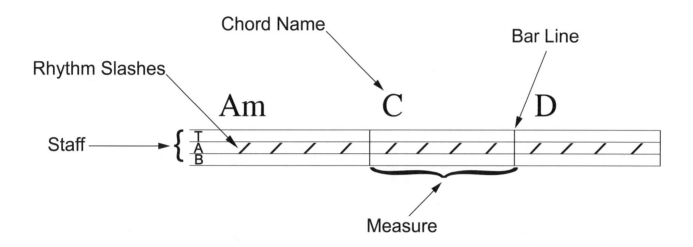

Your First Song

Here is a simple song to put the chords and strumming techniques together. You will be strumming each chord four times using a down stroke. Use your thumb or the felt pick keeping your hand and arm loose.

Strum Pattern

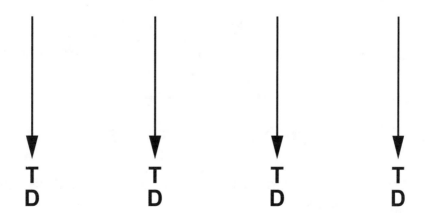

Chords Used

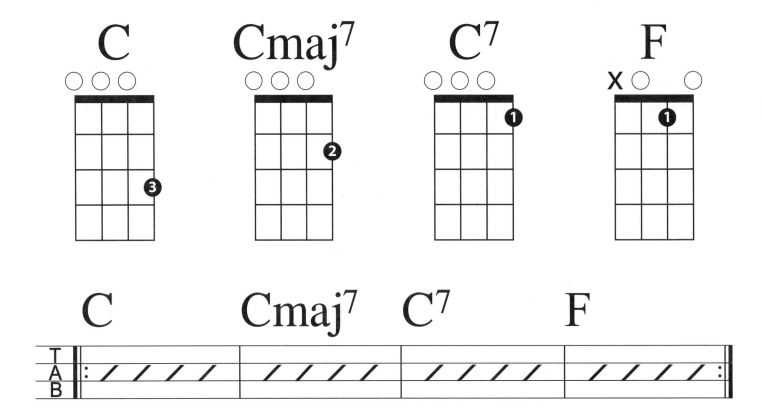

C   Cmaj⁷   C⁷   F

Simile Marks

Simile marks " ℅ " are a form of short-hand writing composers use to show that the preceding groups of beats or measures are to be repeated. In the example here, the simile mark means to repeat the previous measure.

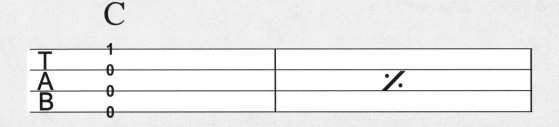

Backing Tracks

Many of the songs in this book will have a backing track that you can play along with. These will be either audio demonstrations or full band tracks. This will help you learn to play with other musicians. The songs can be downloaded using your member number from the *Lesson Support* site.

The G Major Chord

Next lets learn the G Major Chord. Pick each note out individually to make sure the chord sounds clean and all the notes are sounding properly. Notice that when you are fretting this chord your fingers mold into a V shape. Try to notice the finger shape for all your chords this will help you remember them easily.

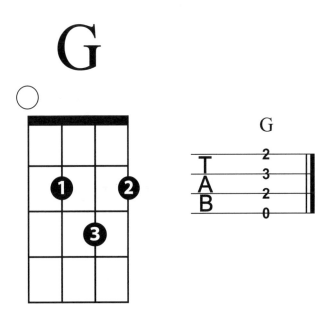

He's Got the Whole World In His Hands

For this progression strum each chord down four times for each measure like you did in the last lesson. Practice changing back and forth between the C and G major chords to develop a smooth transition between the chords.

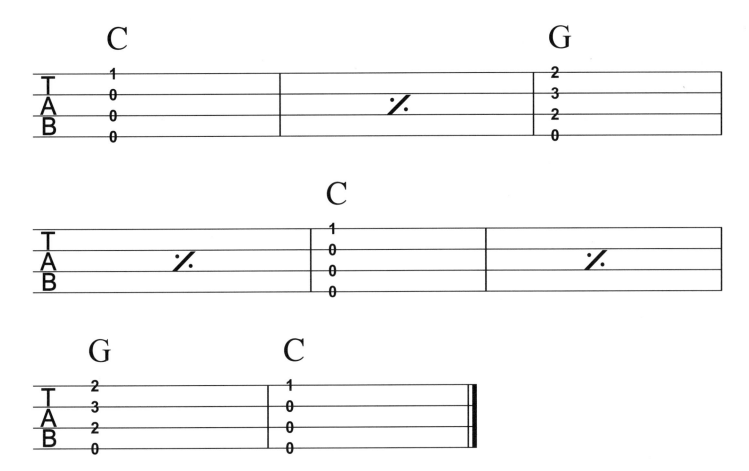

The Musical Alphabet

The musical alphabet consists of seven letters A through G. After G the letters loop back to A and start over again. There are no note names higher in the musical alphabet then G. These seven letters will be the names of the notes on your ukulele.

A - B - C - D - E - F - G

Notes on the First Three Strings

Here are the eight notes on the first three strings. You will be using these to play songs in the upcoming lessons so memorize these notes.

Notes on the C String

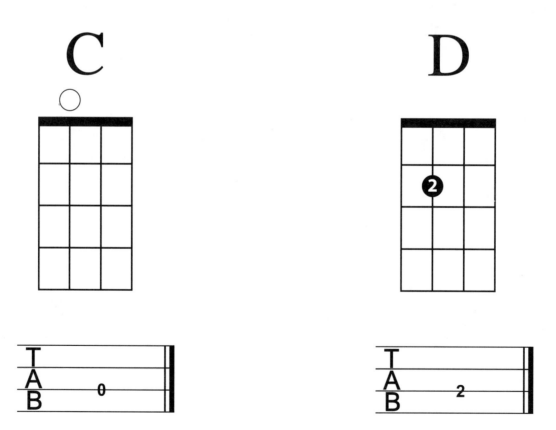

Notes on the E String

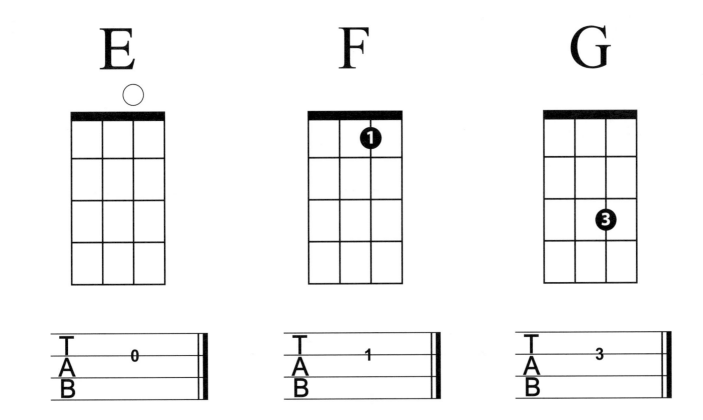

Notes on the A String

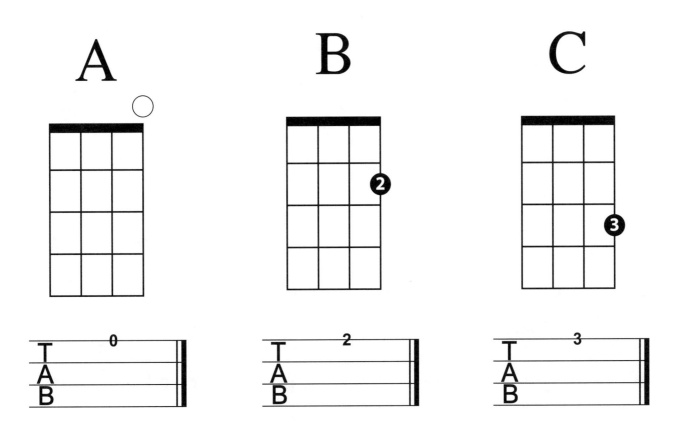

The Major Scale

The notes you learned on the first three strings played in a row create a C major scale. A scale is a group of notes within a key that will work together to create songs. I like to think of a scale as notes within the same family. You will be using these notes in the next lesson to play song melodies.

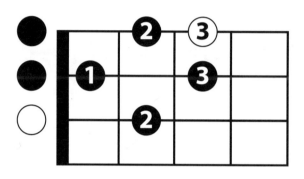

◯ = *Root Note*

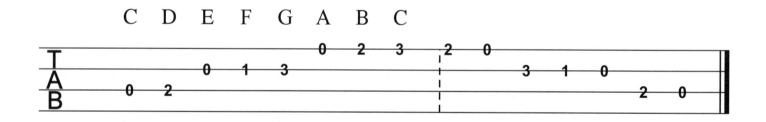

Below is all of the notes of the C major scale on the neck of your ukulele.

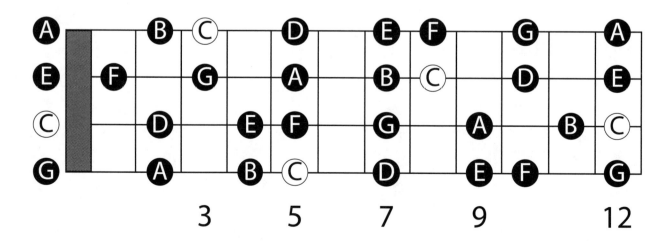

Song Melodies

Here are a few songs using the notes on the first three strings. These notes are also the notes of the C major scale that you just learned. As you play three songs try to say the name of each note out loud. This will help you to memorize the names of the notes on your ukulele.

Aura Lee

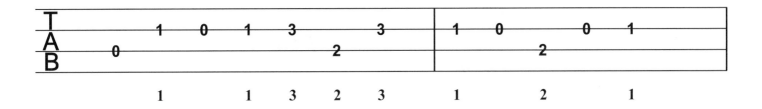

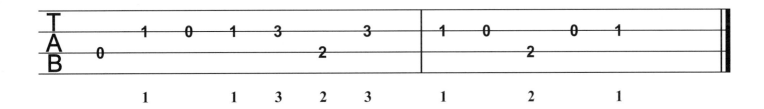

Jingle Bells

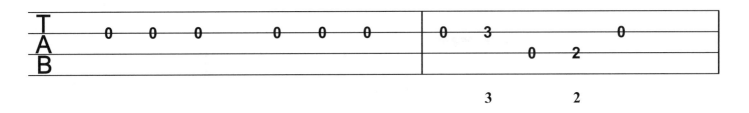

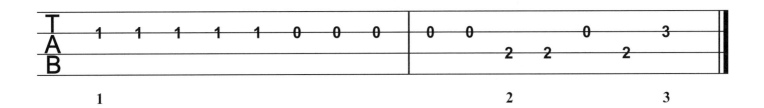

More Chords

Here are some more chords that are commonly found in many songs. Memorize these chords and make sure all the notes are sounded.

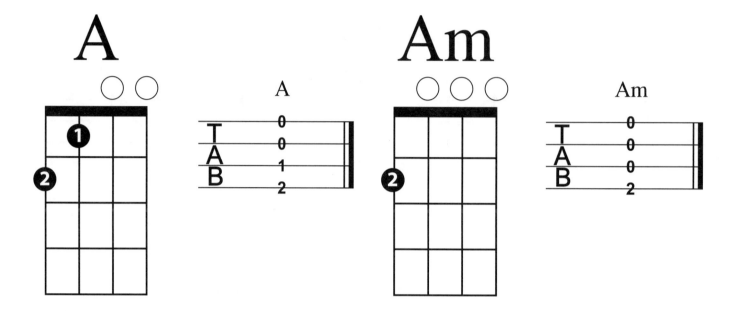

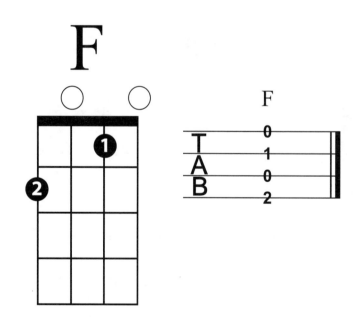

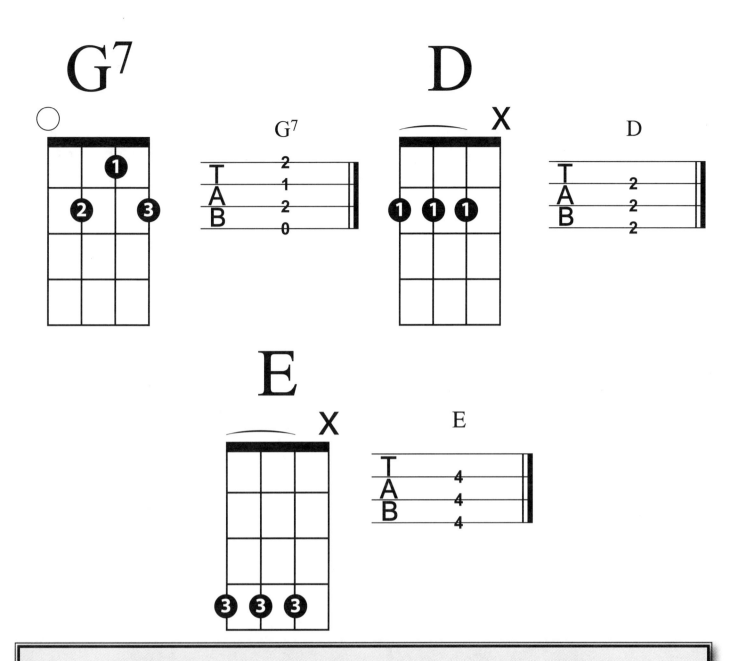

Using the Metronome to Practice

As you progress as a musician you can use the metronome in your daily practice to help keep a steady rhythm and gauge your progress. Here are a few metronome practice tips that will help you use this tool effectively.

1. When starting to learn a new song set the metronome at a slow tempo where you can play the entire piece through without making mistakes.

2. Gradually build your speed by increasing the BPM (beats per minute) on the metronome a few numbers each day.

3. As you play with the metronome try not to focus on it too much. Sense the feel of the click and concentrate on the song you are playing.

Complete Song Progressions

Here are two complete songs using the chords you have learned so far. Start off slowly and build up to tempo gradually. Once you feel comfortable with the chord changes play the songs along with the backing track and have some fun.

Strum Pattern - Use this pattern once for each measure

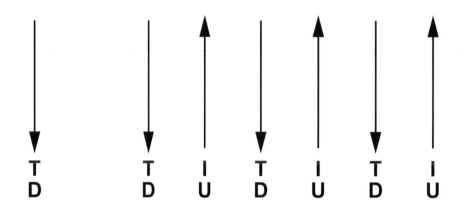

Chords Used

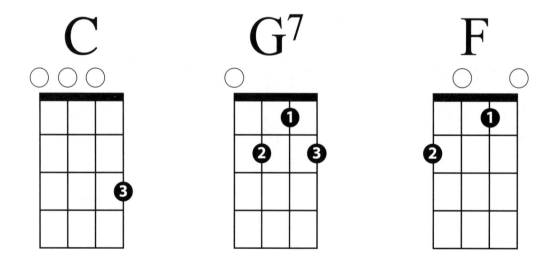

Repeat Signs

In music, a repeat sign is a sign that indicates a section should be repeated. If the piece has one repeat sign alone (end repeat), then that means to repeat from the beginning, and then continue on (or stop, if the sign appears at the end of the piece). A corresponding sign facing the other way (start repeat) indicates where the repeat is to begin.

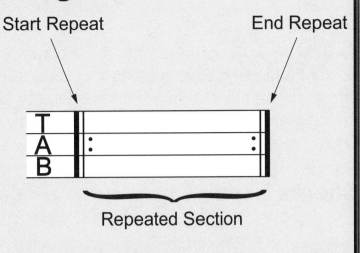

Start Repeat

End Repeat

Repeated Section

Oh When the Saints

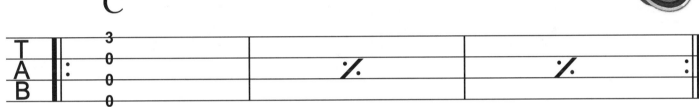

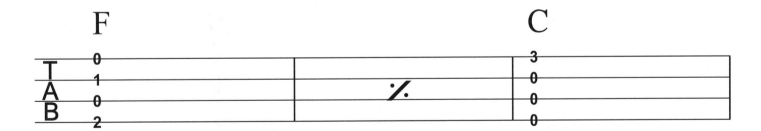

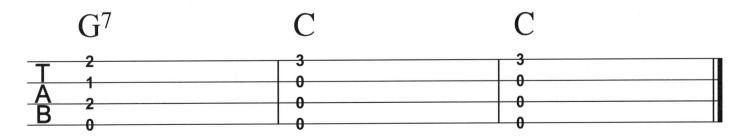

The 1 - 4 - 5 Progression

The I – IV – V chords are the most common chord combination in all music. Many hit songs have been written using this song structure. It is called a I – IV – V progression because you build chords from the 1st, 4th and 5th notes in the major scale. Below are the diagrams for all three chords. Play them one after another and hear the sound of this chord progression.

Chords Used

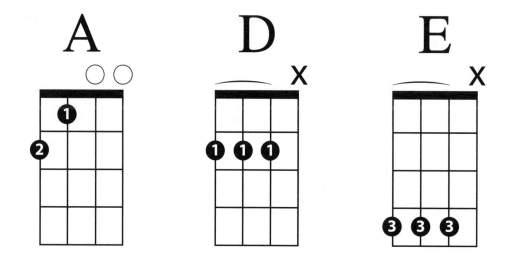

Strum Pattern

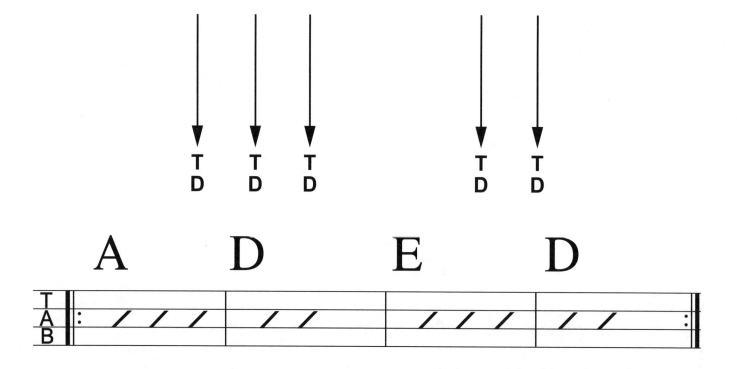

Song Melodies

Here are a few more song melodies to learn. Have fun!

Oh When the Saints

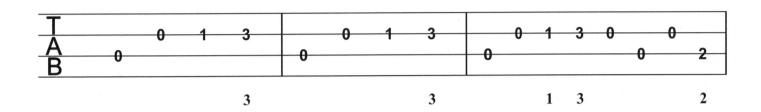

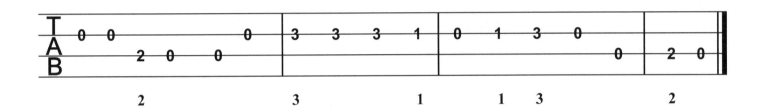

Kum-Ba-Ya

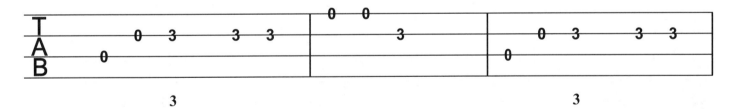

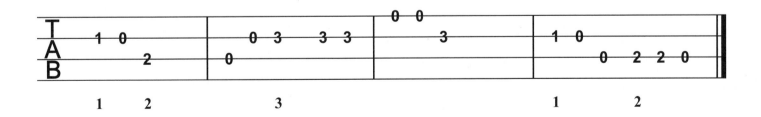

Ode to Joy

Here is a great classical melody by Beethoven. Notice the curved line connecting three notes on the 3rd staff. This indicates that these notes will be played quickly in a row. Take your time and practice this song section by section and then put it all together with the backing track.

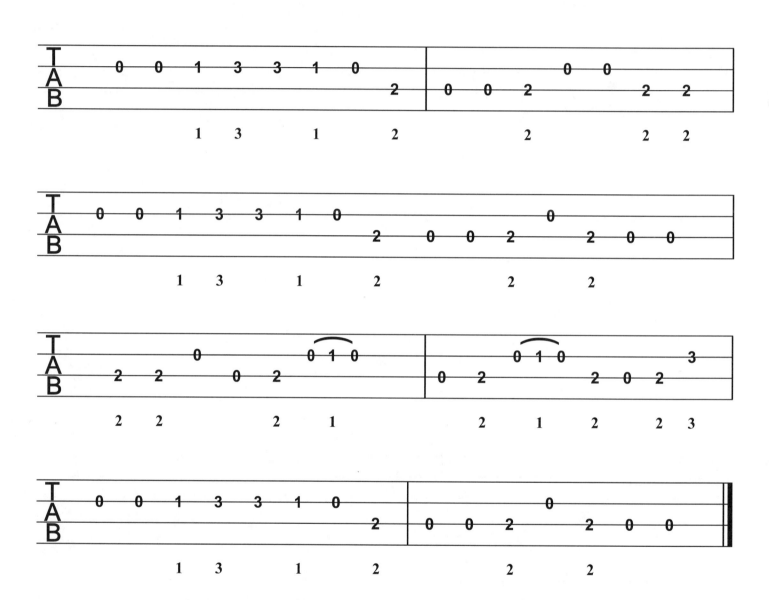

Blues in the Key of "A"

Blues has influenced almost every genre of music. The following is a 12 bar blues progressions constructed using the 1 – 4 and 5 chords. It is called 12 bar blues because it contains 12 measures before repeating to the beginning.

Strum Pattern

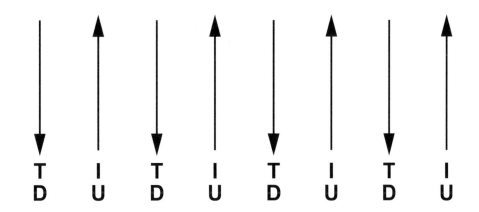

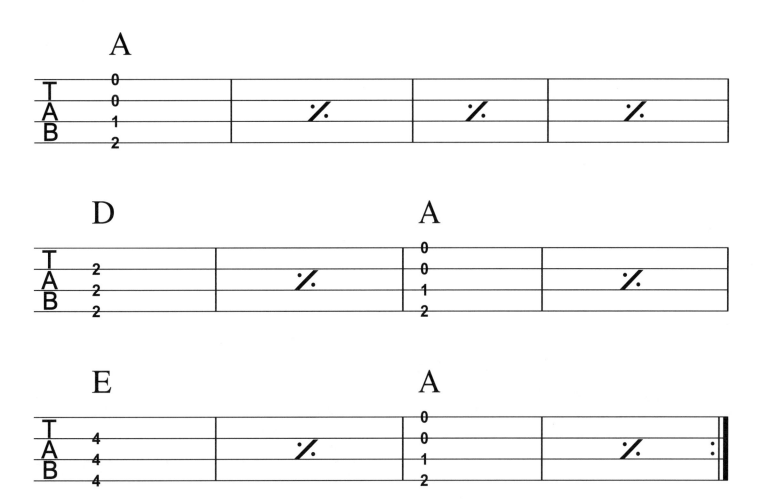

Vibrato

Vibrato is the small, fast shaking of a note. Vibrato is indicated by a squiggly line above the staff, extending out above a note. While letting a note ring, shake your finger slightly and dig into the note slightly and vibrate the pitch to give it more expression.

Twinkle, Twinkle Little Star

First Section

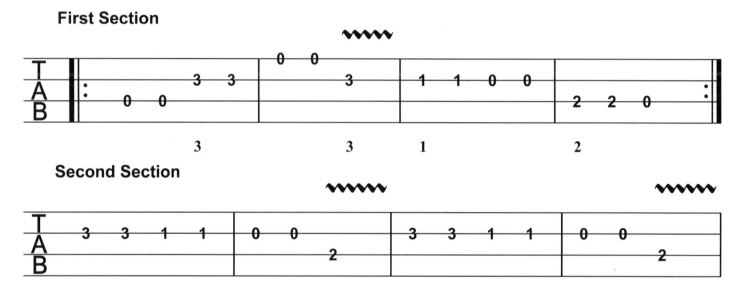

Second Section

Third Section

Learn Ukulele - Quiz 2

Once you complete this section go to RockHouseMethod.com and take the quiz to track your progress. You will receive an email with your results and suggestions.

House of the Rising Sun

Here is a great song rhythm that uses many of the chords you have learned with the addition of three new chords: the Am, D major and the E major. The strum pattern is complicated so pay close attention to the symbols below.

Strum Pattern - Use this pattern once for each measure

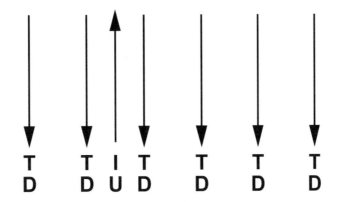

Chords Used

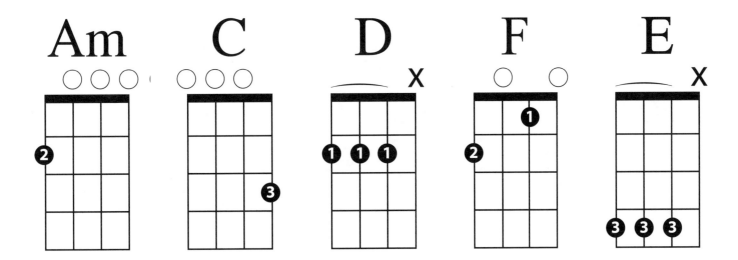

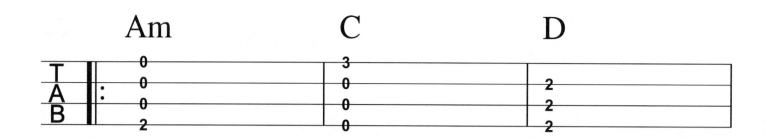

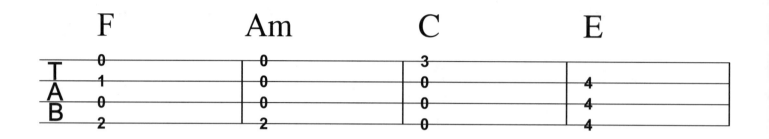

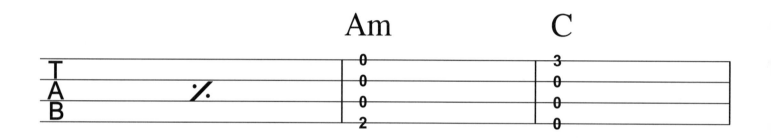

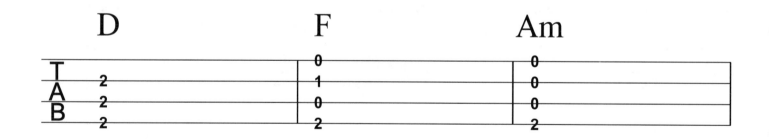

The Minor Scale

Just like there are major and minor chords there are major and minor scales. Major has the bright happy sound while minor has a sad melancholy tone.

C Minor Scale

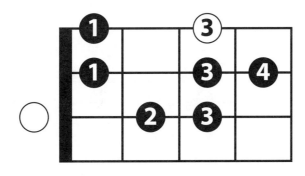

 = *Root Note*

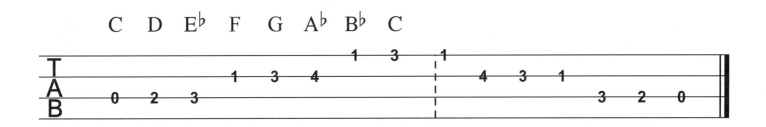

Below is all of the notes of the C minor scale on the neck of your ukulele.

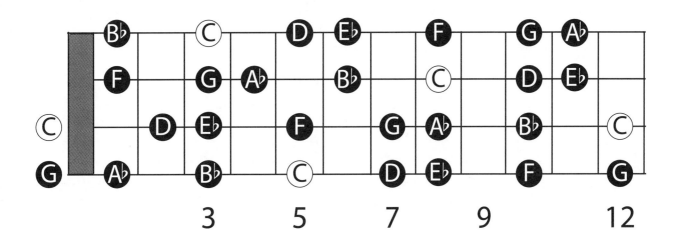

D Minor Scale

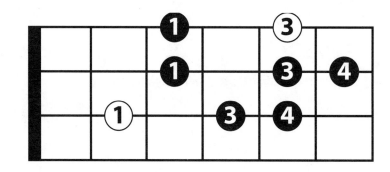

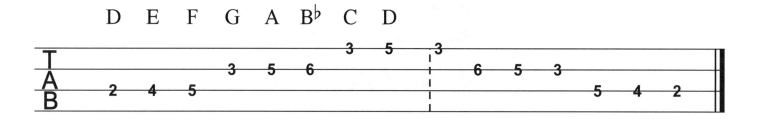

Finger Exercises

Here is a finger exercise to help develop the coordination of your fingers. Start slow and build up speed gradually. This is a great exercise to use a metronome with to help gauge your progress.

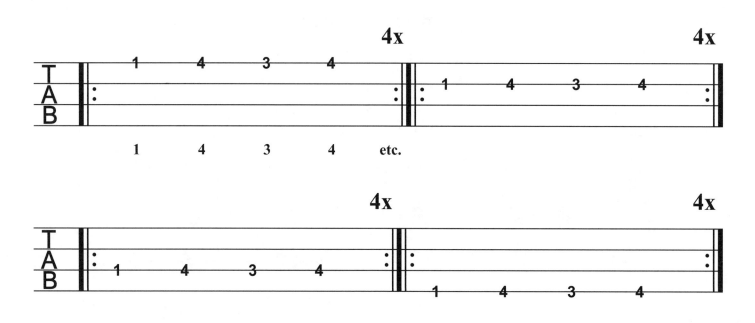

Minor and Seventh Chords

Let's learn some more chords. The more chords you know the more songs you will be able to play so work hard on these chords and memorize them all.

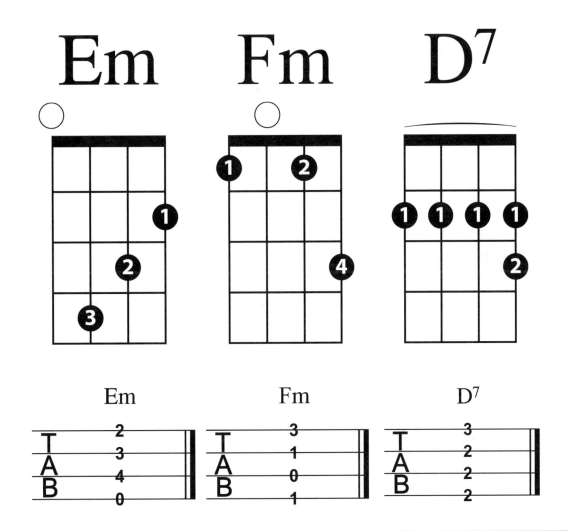

Em

```
T    2
A  3
B  4
     0
```

Fm

```
T    3
A  1
B  0
     1
```

D⁷

```
T    3
A  2
B  2
     2
```

Practice Tips

To ensure constant progress and high motivation you have to develop practice habits that will keep you interested and challenged. Here are a few tips:

Practice Consistently - You need to give your fingers a chance to gain muscle memory. Practice every day even if it is for a short amount of time, be consistent.

Practice Area - Have a practice spot set up so you can have privacy to focus on your playing. It is a great idea to have a music stand to help position your music so you can sit comfortably.

Practice Schedule - Set a scheduled practice time each day and make this a routine. Other times in the day you can play for fun and jam a little.

Strumming Variations

Strumming patterns can give a song a unique sound. Here are a few popular strum variations. Apply these strum patterns to the new chords you just learned in the previous lesson. Remember to keep your arm lose and relaxed to get a smooth strum rhythm feel.

Strum Pattern #1

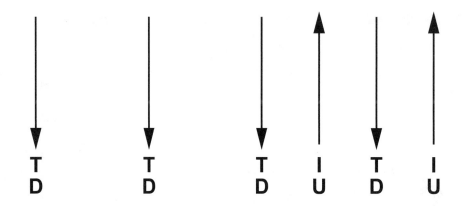

Strum Pattern #2

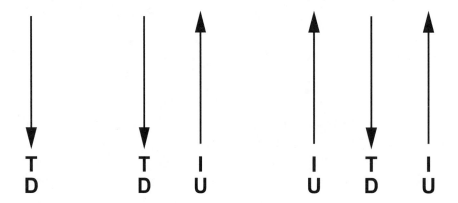

The Rainbow Song

This is a familiar sounding chord progression with many chord changes. Practice changing from chord to chord before playing the whole progression, this will help you to have quick transitions and a seamless overall sound.

Strum Pattern - Use this pattern once for each measure

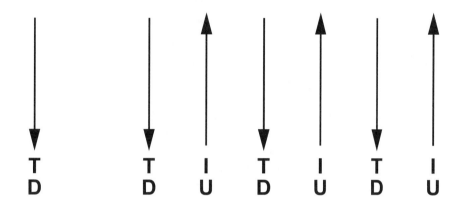

Chords Used

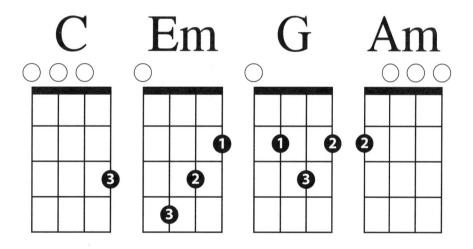

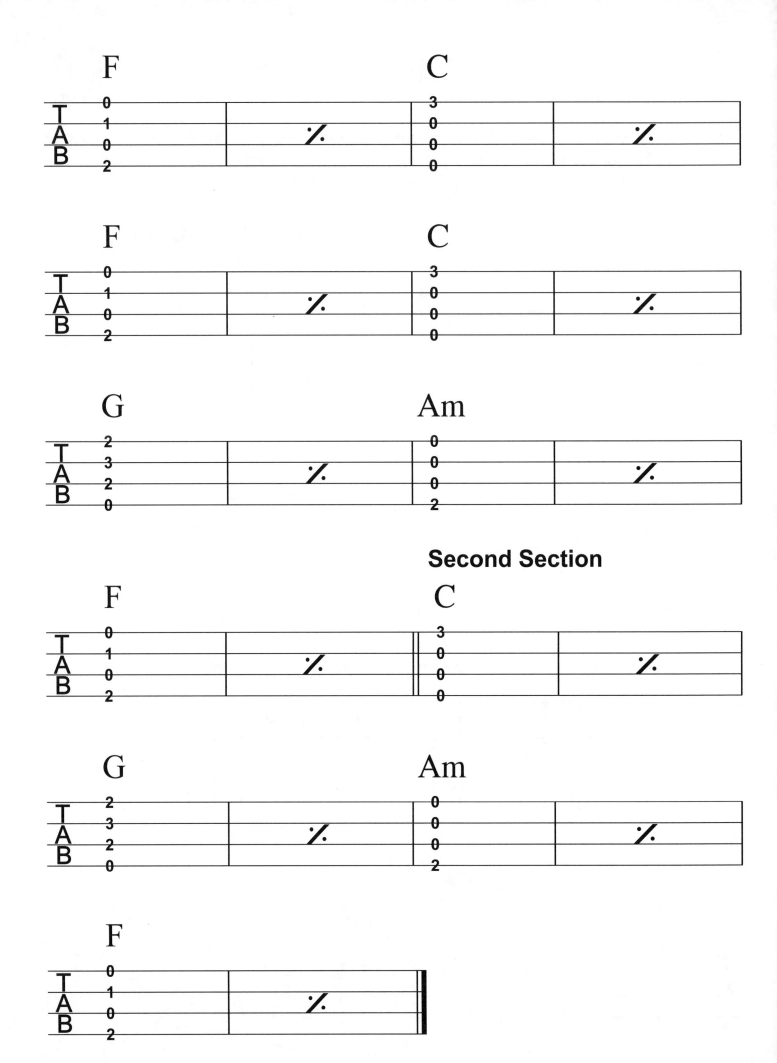

Second Section

Finger Picking Progression

Songs can be played by picking out chords, strumming them or a combination of both. Here is a chord progression using a picking pattern to help you get familiar with this technique.

Chords Used

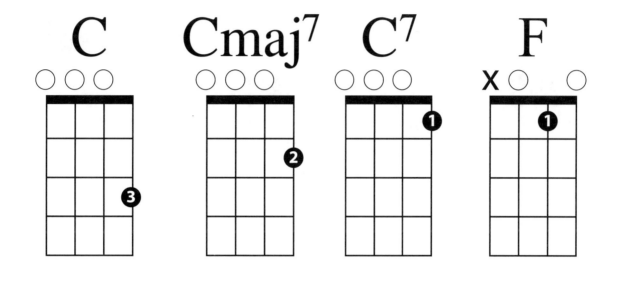

C   Cmaj⁷   C⁷   F

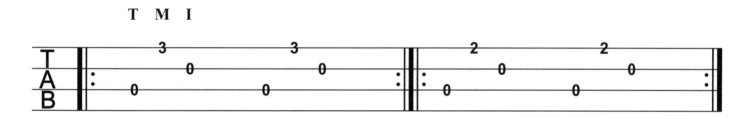

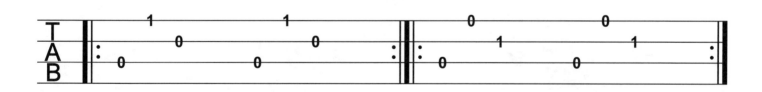

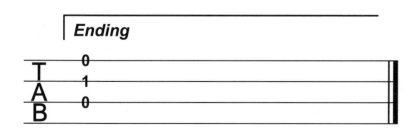

Ending

T = Thumb
M = Middle Finger
I = Index Finger

The Fingernail Rake

The fingernail rake is a popular technique for the ukulele. There are two variations of this technique that I will cover in this lesson. The first uses your index finger tip and nail to quickly move up and down the four strings repetitively. This technique is a great way to create a climax in a song.

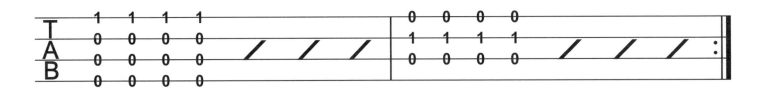

The second way the finger nail rake is played is by fanning the four fingers on your picking hand across the strings starting with the pinky to the index finger. With this technique you get four quick strums one as each finger crosses the strings.

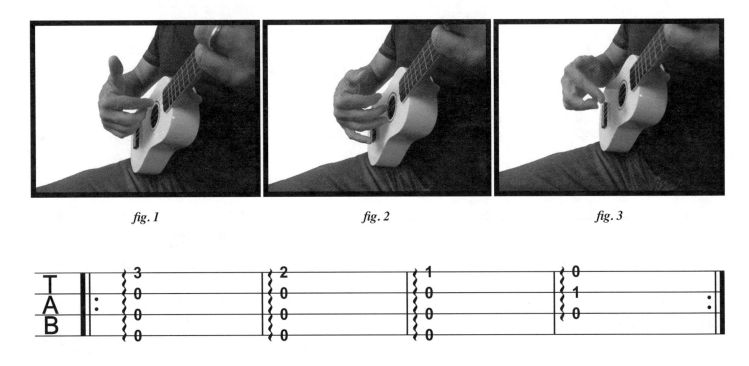

fig. 1   fig. 2   fig. 3

Here are a few more song melodies that are fun to play. They are very popular melodies so they should sound familiar.

This Land Is Your Land

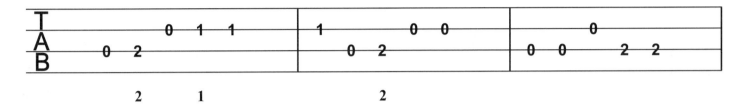

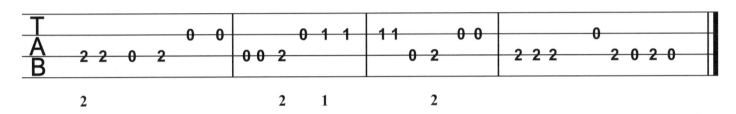

Oh Susanna

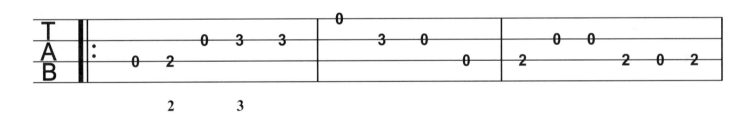

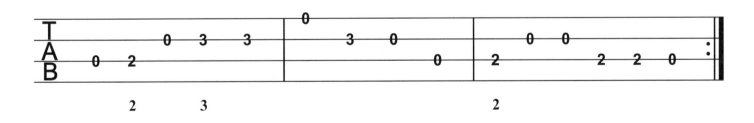

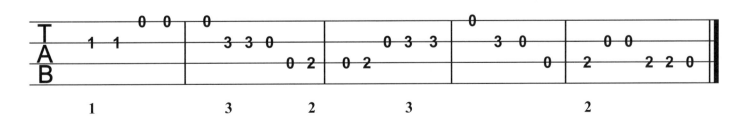

Oh When the Saints Variation

A turnaround is a section that comes at the end of a progression that brings the song back to the beginning. Here is a turnaround that you can add to Oh When the Saints that you previously learned.

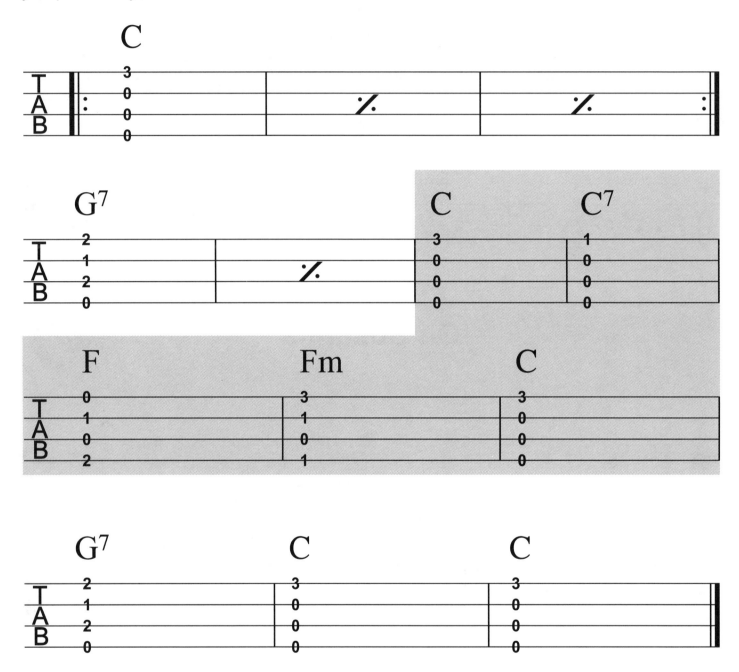

Minor Pentatonic Scales Key of "A"

Minor pentatonic scales are the most widely used scale in rock and blues music. It is a five note scale ("penta" meaning five) containing the notes A – C – D – E – G.

Position 1   ## Position 2

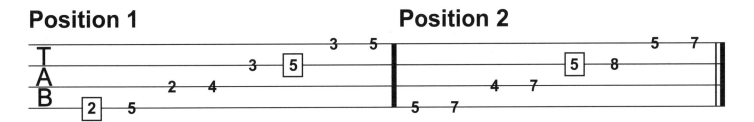

Position 3   ## Position 4

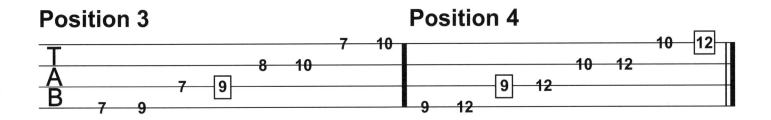

Position 5

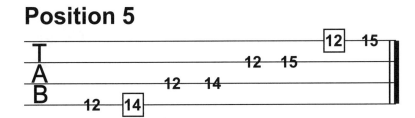

Below is all of the notes of the A minor pentatonic scale on the neck of your ukulele.

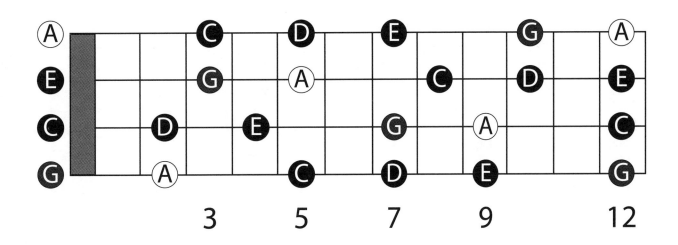

Lead Techniques Bending

Bending is a widely used technique for the ukulele. It is a great way to add soul and emotional dimension to your note's. To bend a note simply pick it and push your finger up while keeping the pressure down. By doing this you alter and control the notes pitch. An arrow above a note indicates a bend, the word "full" at the end of the arrow indicates a whole step bend. When fretting the bend keep the other fingers down to help give strength, control and accuracy.

Example 1   Example 2

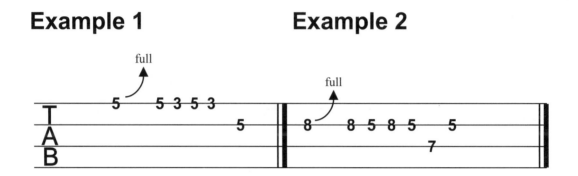

Lead Techniques Hammer-ons

Hammer-ons are a commonly used technique. A curved line connecting two notes with an "H" on top indicates a hammer-on. Pick the first note; the second note will be sounded by pushing your finger down in a hammer like fashion to make the sound resonate.

Example 1   Example 2

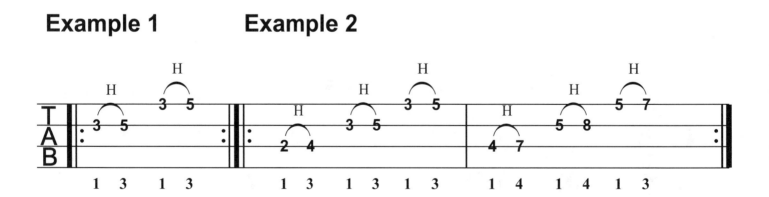

Lead Techniques Pull-offs

Pull-offs are the opposite of hammer-ons. A curved line connecting two notes with a "P" on top indicates a pull-off. Pick the first note; the second note will be sounded by snapping, or pulling, your finger off to make the second note resonate.

Example 1   **Example 2**

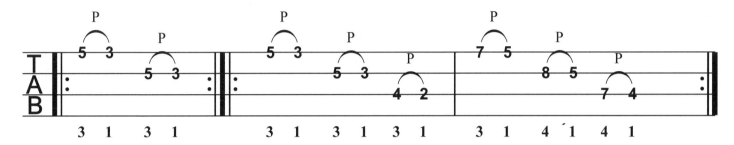

Blues Riffs

The following are a series of riffs created from the minor pentatonic scales in the key of "A". After you have mastered each apply them over the Blues in "A" backing track and have some fun.

Example 1   **Example 2**

Example 3   **Example 4**

Example 5

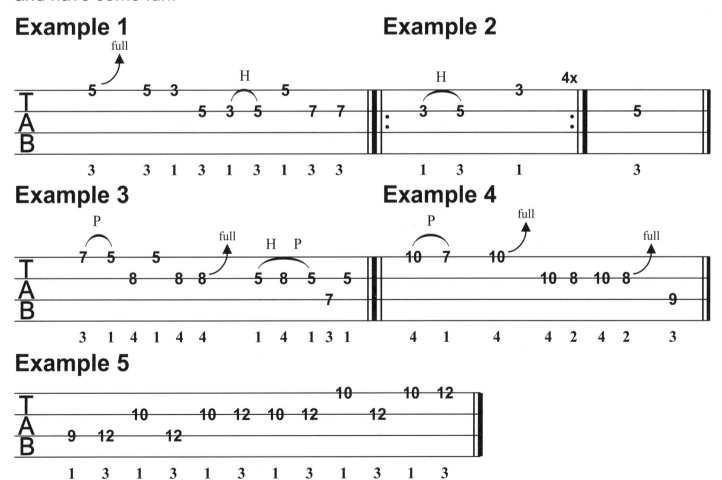

The 4 Chord Song

1 – 5 – 6 – 4 Progression Key of "C"

The 1 – 5 – 6 – 4 progression is today's most popular chord progression being used in thousands of songs. Once you have learned this progression you will be able to play many songs, so get excited!

Strum Pattern - Use this pattern once for each measure

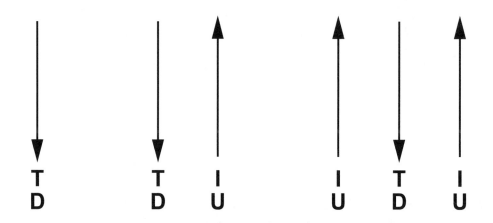

T	T	I	I	T	I
D	D	U	U	D	U

Chords Used

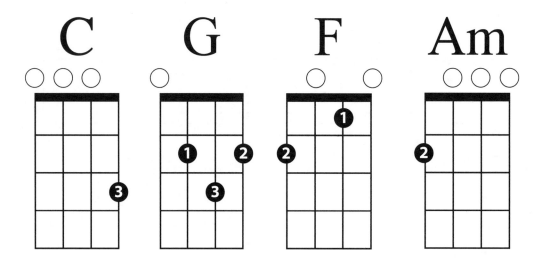

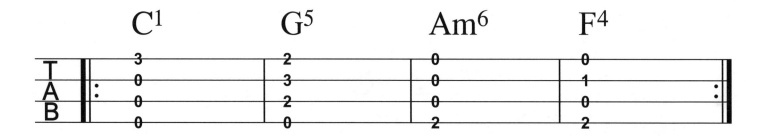

The 4 Chord Song Part 2
1 – 6 – 4 – 5 Progression Key of "C"

This is another very common song progression made famous in the 50's and 60's with songs like "In the Still of the Night" and "Stand by Me". It also has been used throughout the years by many artists and even in today's music. Notice how it used the same chords from the 1 – 5 – 6 – 4 progression just in a different order giving it a unique sound.

Strum Pattern - Use this pattern once for each measure

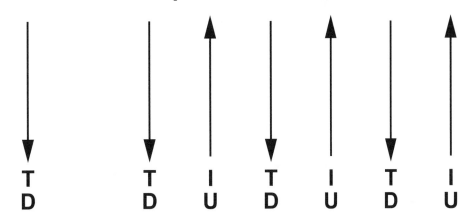

Chords Used

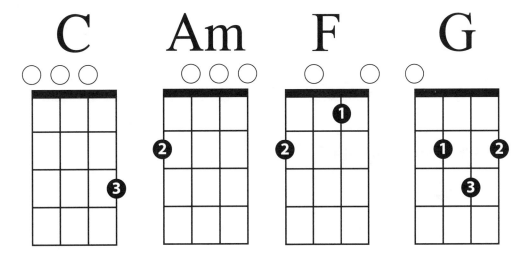

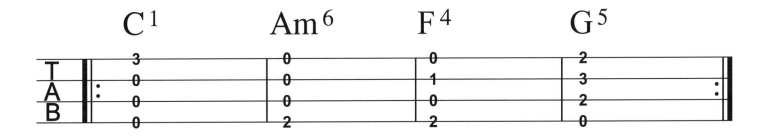

Epic Sun

1 – 5 – 6 – 4 Progression Key of "G"

Now you will learn a 1 – 5 – 6 – 4 progression in the key of "G". Make sure to practice the chord changes back and forth to help get muscle memory and quick chord changes. The strum pattern for this song progression is down – down-up – up-down-up.

Strum Pattern - Use this pattern once for each measure

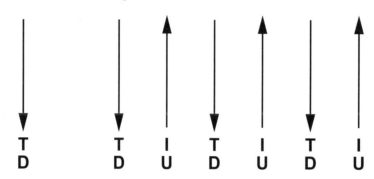

Chords Used

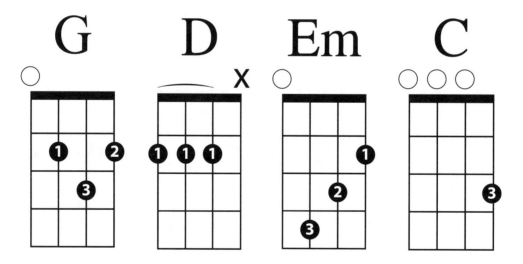

Black Pearl

6 – 2 – 5 – 3 Progression Key of "C"

This is a minor song progression. The first chord is Am which is the relative minor to C major. Many minor song progressions begin on the relative minor chord. Also in this progression are the Dm and Em chords. The strum pattern for this song is down – down-up-down-up-down.

Strum Pattern - Use this pattern once for each measure

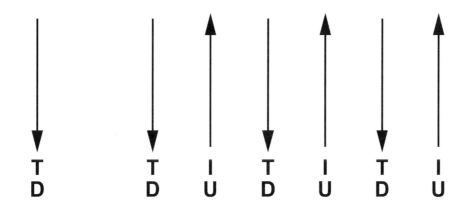

T	T	I	T	I	T	I
D	D	U	D	U	D	U

Chords Used

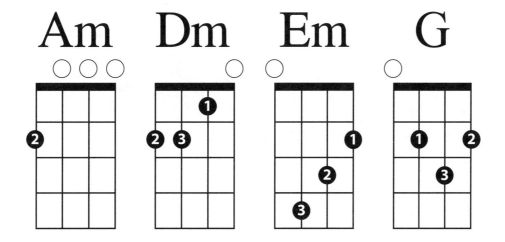

Street of Dreams

2 – 4 – 1 – 5 Progression Key of "D"

This is another popular song progression. Notice how the 1 – 4 – 5 chords are in here but also included is the 2 chord which is Em. The strum pattern for this song is down – down – down – down-up.

Strum Pattern - Use this pattern once for each measure

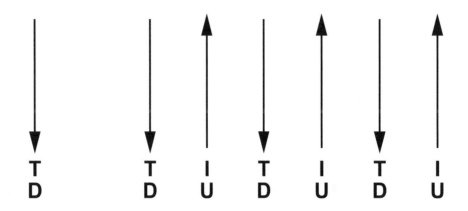

T		T	I	T	I	T	I
D		D	U	D	U	D	U

Chords Used

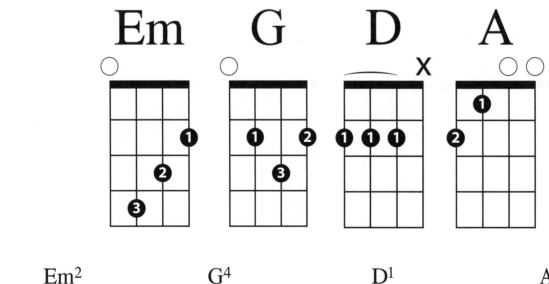

Em²   G⁴   D¹   A⁵

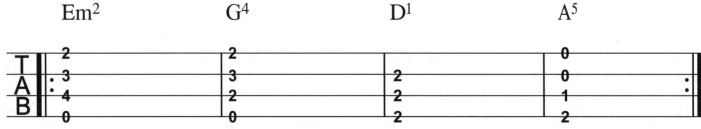

Finger Picking Blues

The following is an "A" 1 – 4 – 5 blues progression using 7th chords. The finger-picking string pattern is 3 – 1 – 4 – 2 using the fingers P – M – P – I for each chord. The last section is a turnaround that incorporates a slide. Practice this slowly and build your speed gradually.

Chords Used

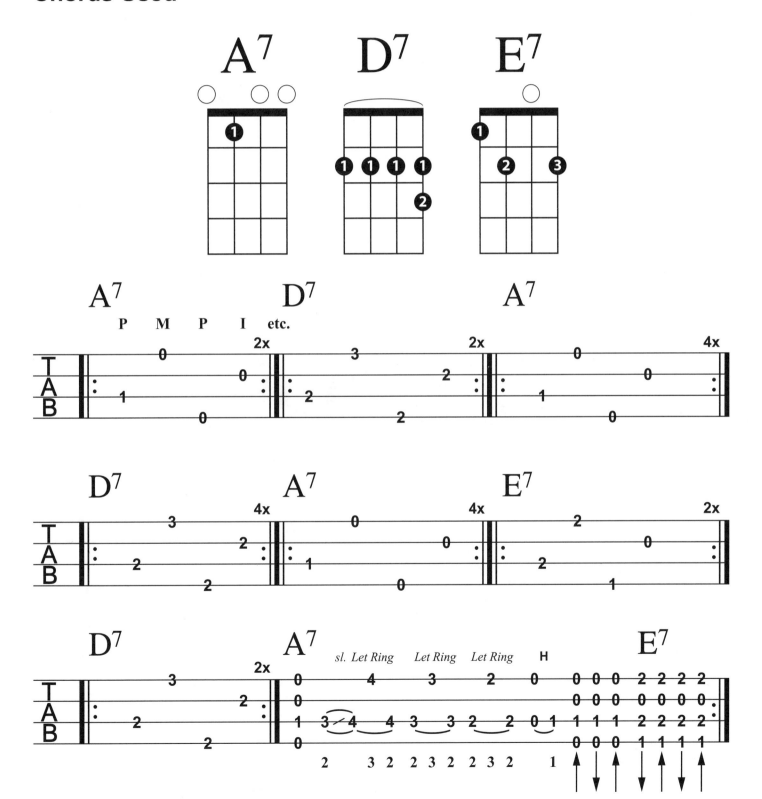

Learn Ukulele - Quiz 3

Once you complete this section go to RockHouseMethod.com and take the quiz to track your progress. You will receive an email with your results and suggestions.

Appendix

Chord Dictionary

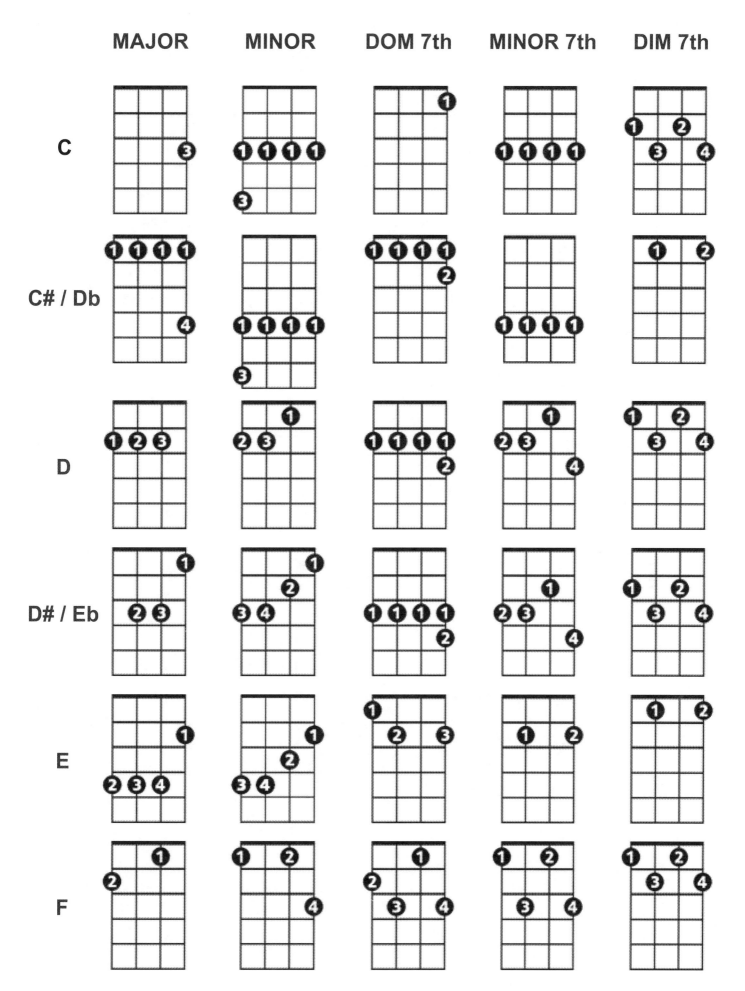

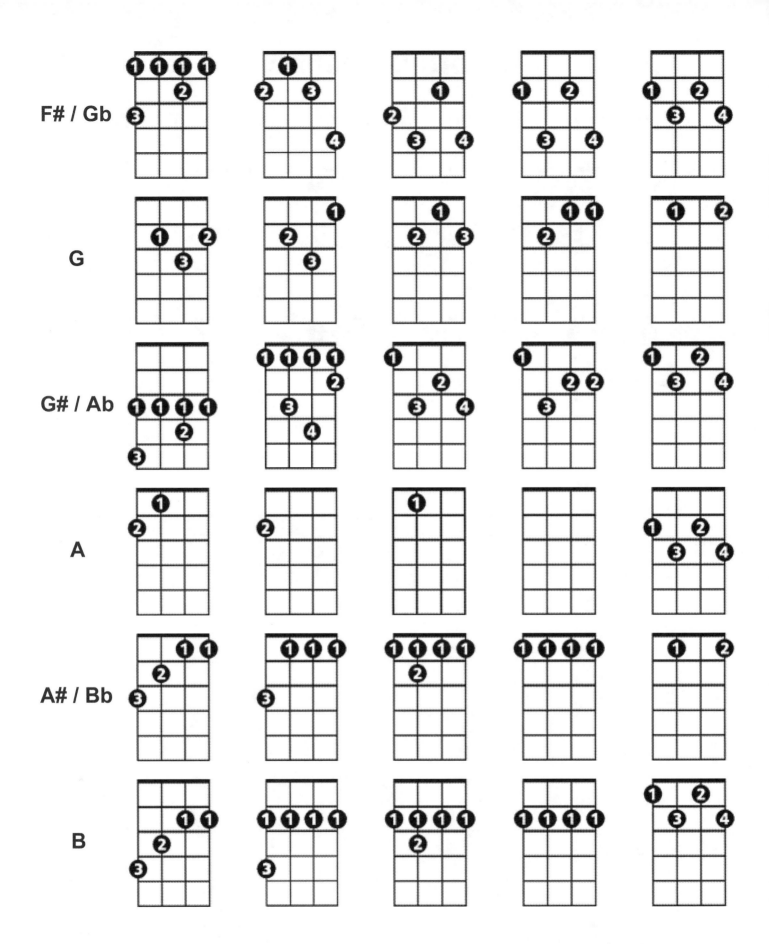

F# / Gb

G

G# / Ab

A

A# / Bb

B

Common Strum Patterns

Strum Pattern #1

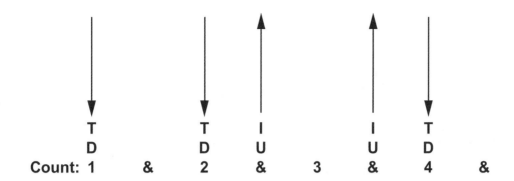

Strum Pattern #2

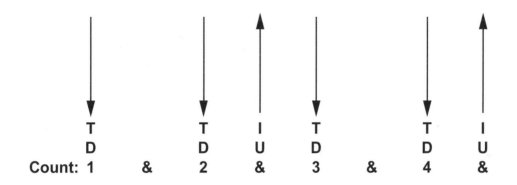

Strum Pattern #3

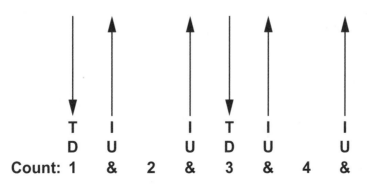

Strum Pattern #4

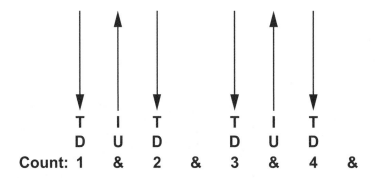

Strum Pattern #5

This is a two measure long pattern.

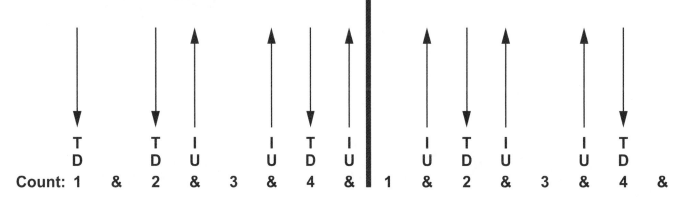

Strum Pattern #6

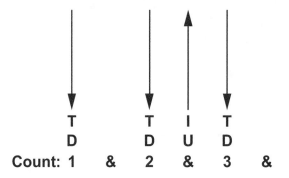

Strum Pattern #7

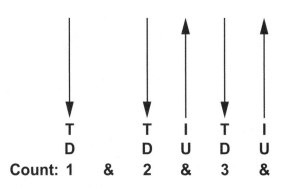

Major Scale Dictionary

C Major

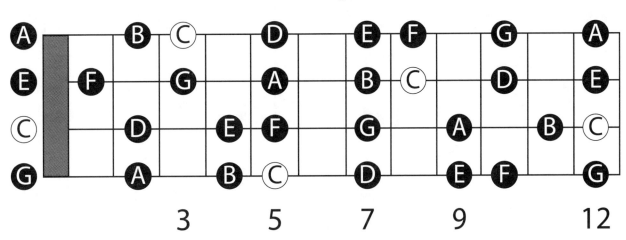

3   5   7   9   12

G Major

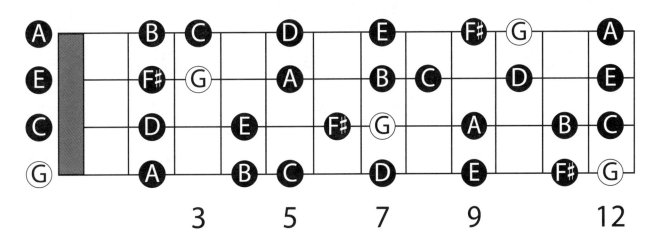

3   5   7   9   12

D Major

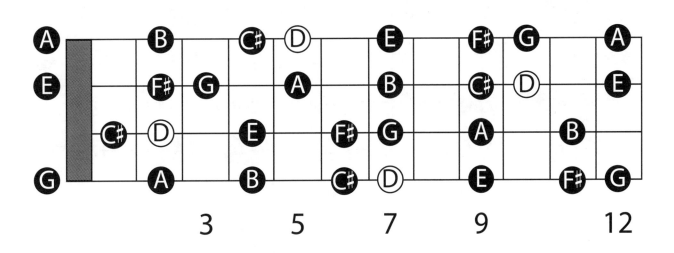

3   5   7   9   12

A Major

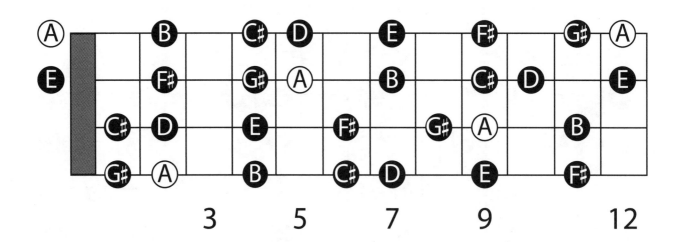

E Major

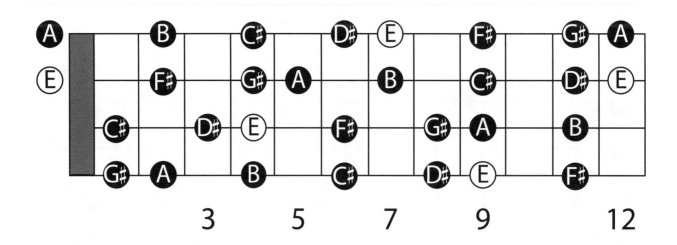

B Major

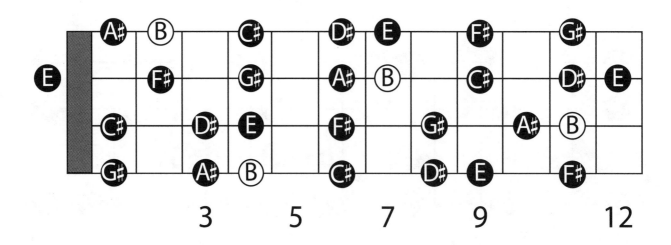

F# Major

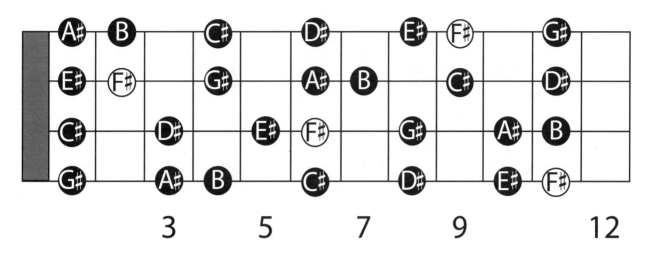

C# Major

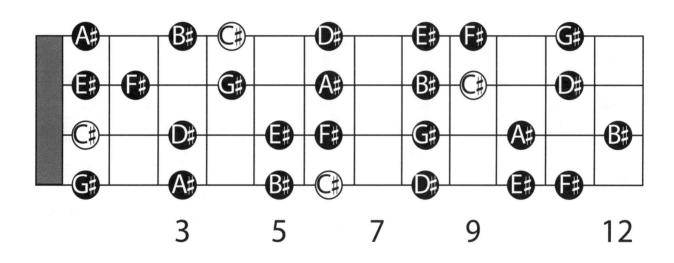

Gb Major

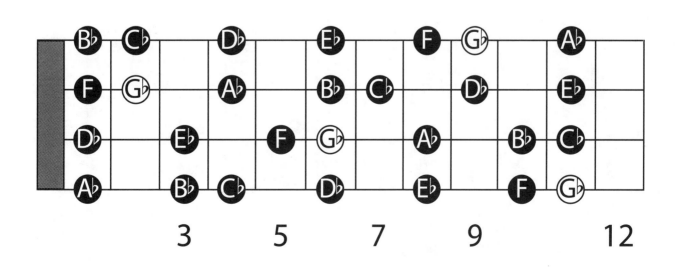

Db Major

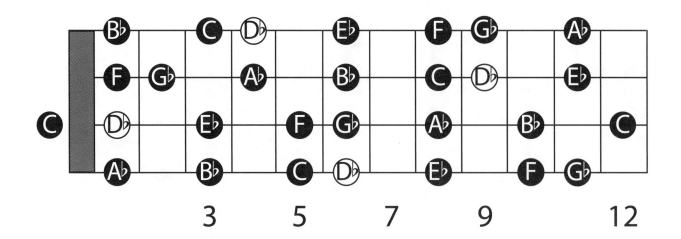

Ab Major

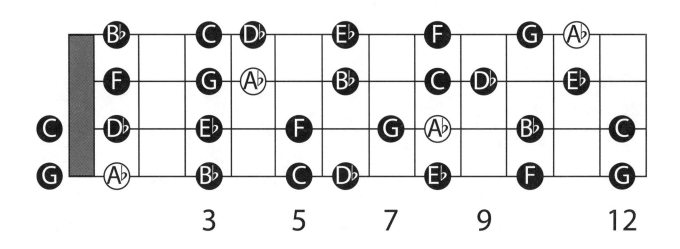

Eb Major

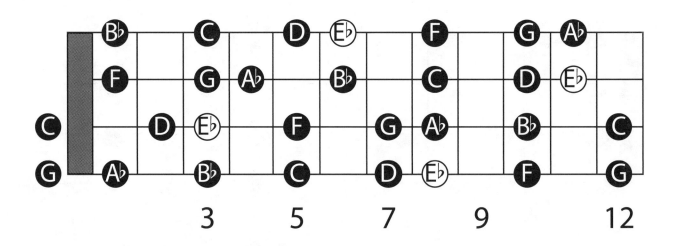

Bb Major

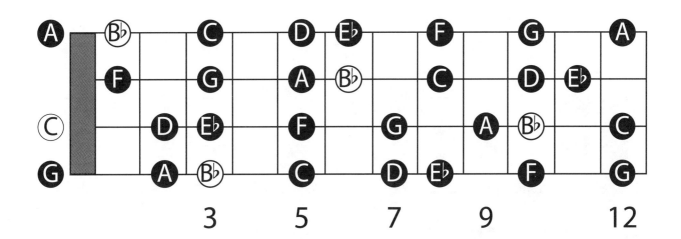

F Major

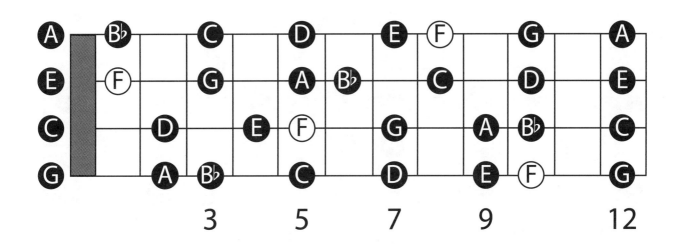

Minor Scale Dictionary

C Minor

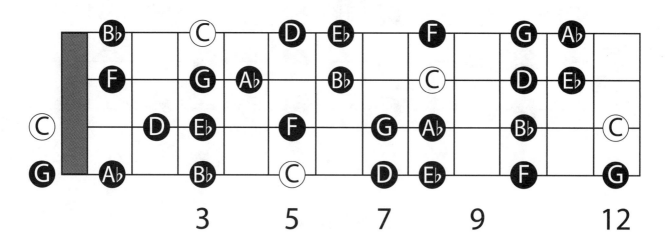

G Minor

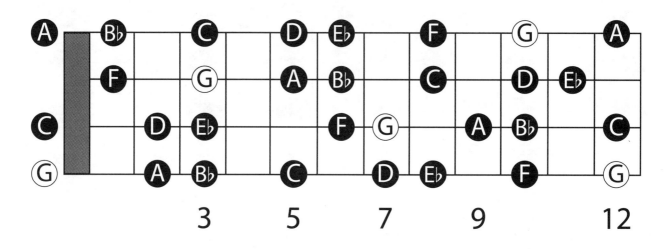

D Minor

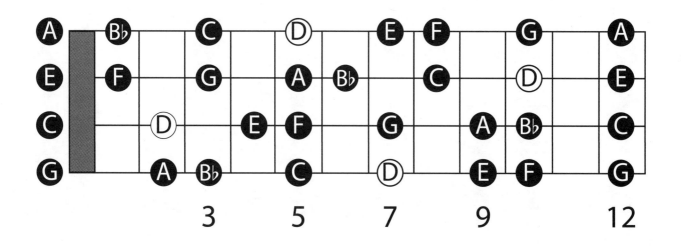

A Minor

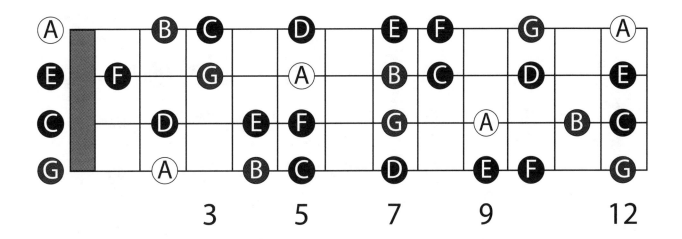

E Minor

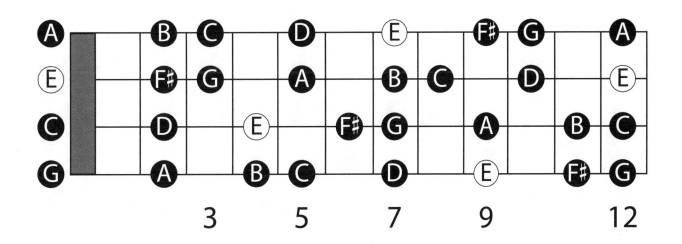

B Minor

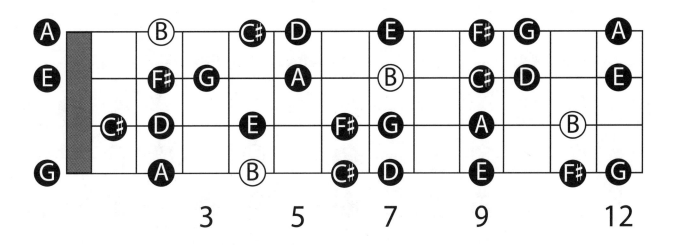

F# Minor

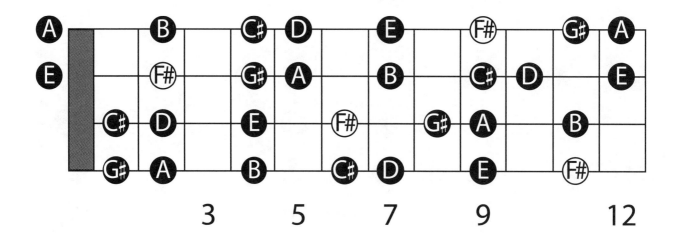

C# Minor

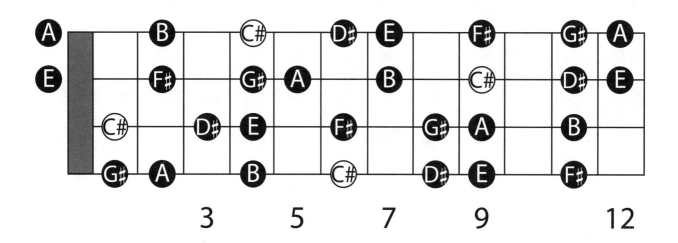

G# Minor

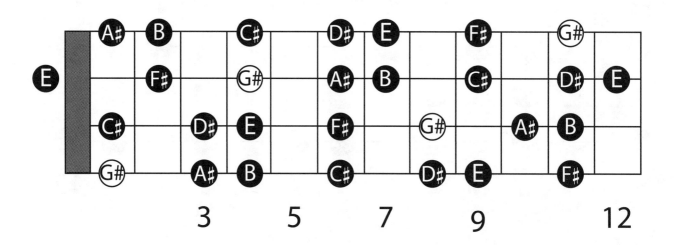

Eb Minor

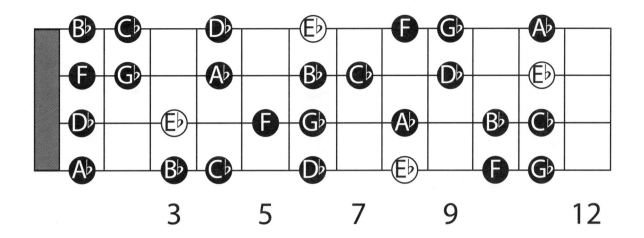

Bb Minor

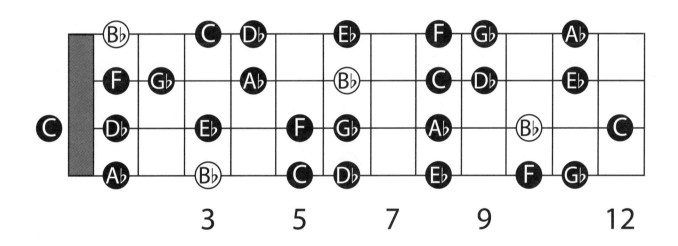

F Minor

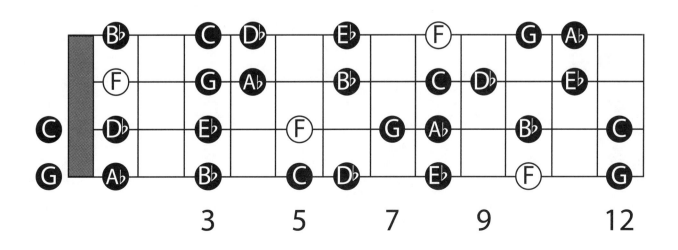

Minor Pentatonic Scale Dictionary

C Minor Pentatonic

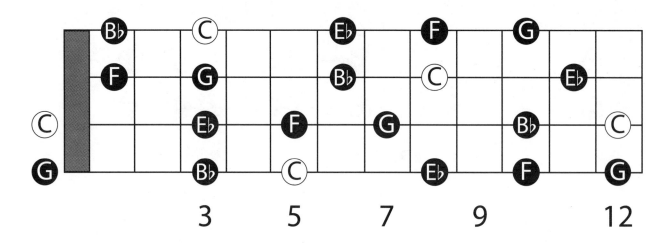

G Minor Pentatonic

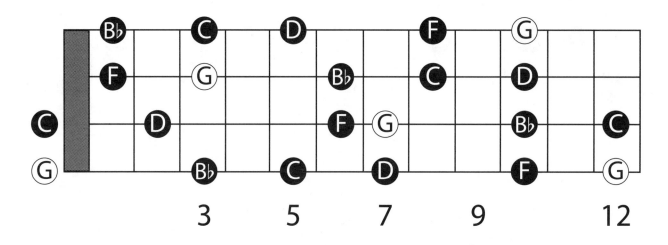

D Minor Pentatonic

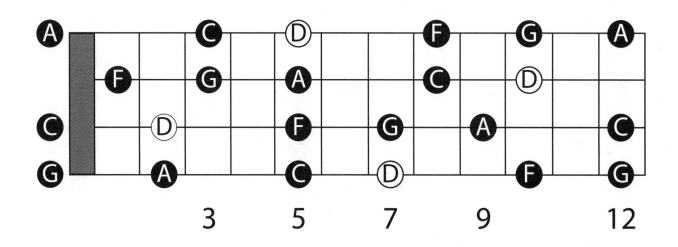

A Minor Pentatonic

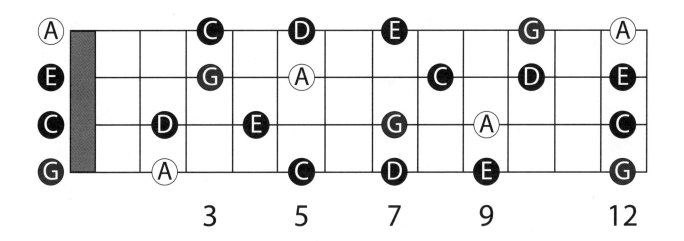

E Minor Pentatonic

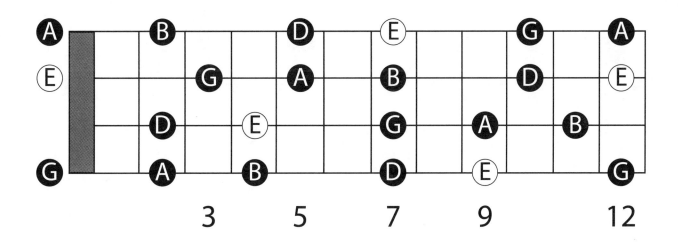

B Minor Pentatonic

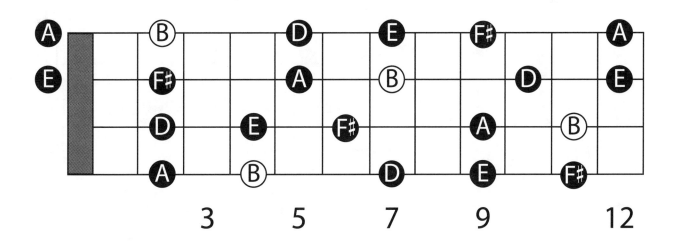

F# Minor Pentatonic

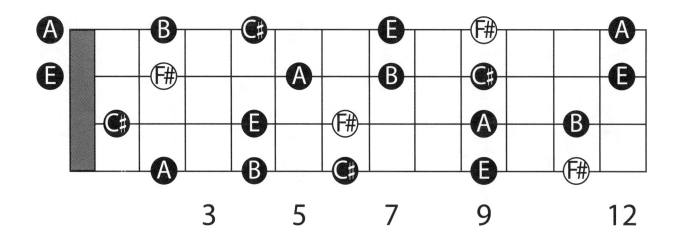

C# Minor Pentatonic

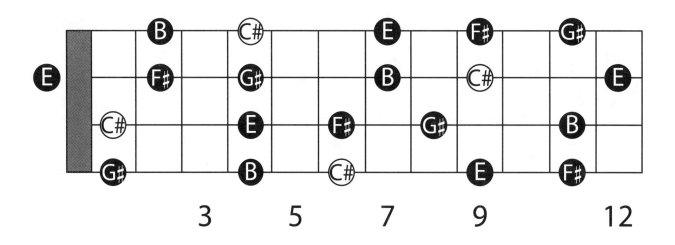

G# Minor Pentatonic

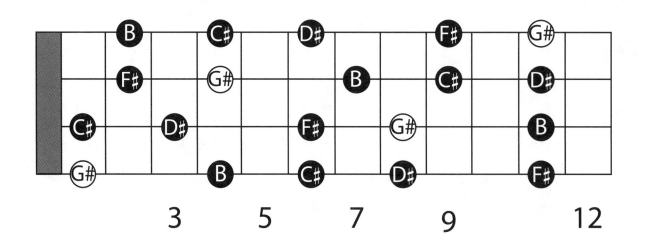

Eb Minor Pentatonic

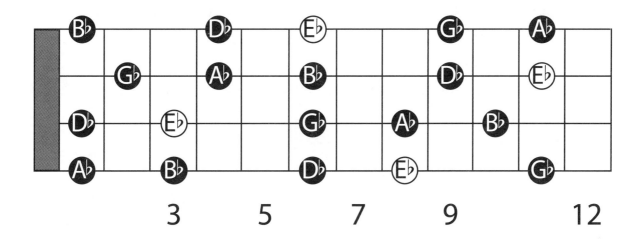

Bb Minor Pentatonic

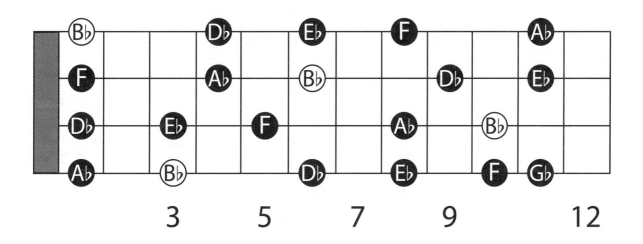

F Minor Pentatonic

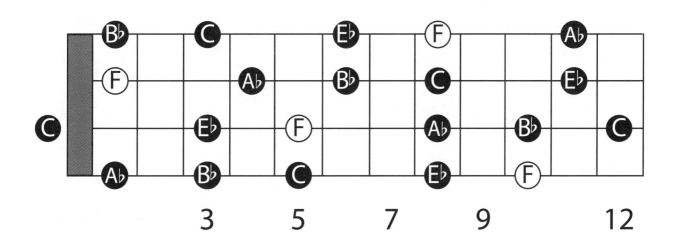

Word Search Puzzle

Go to RockHouseMethod.com to get the answers to this puzzle.

```
G H P E J U N N L R B M U S M
G N R E S M V O F I I O K V A
Y N I Z N I H C D N F R W I J
H P S K V T C T O U A G E B O
T H A K C Y A R Y M D N T R R
R G A T D I S T E H O I O A S
A W N O T C P I O X R R N T C
C J L O A E L R T N E T T O A
C E V L S I R W E U I S O C L
M Z E B M R P N F G N C O H E
N I I I A W A H M W N E R O W
H E S U O H K C O R I I R R Q
O P R O G R E S S I O N F D C
J U K E L E L E S T R U M A I
M J H U R I B T E Y B K C I P
```

Word Search Key

Chord	Rhythm
Exercise	Rock House
Finger Picking	Root Note
Hawaii	Scale
John McCarthy	Similie Marks
Major Scale	Song
Melody	String
Minor Scale	Strum
Pattern	Tuner
Pentatonic	Ukelele
Pick	Vibrato
Progression	

About the Author

John McCarthy
Creator of
The Rock House Method

John is the creator of **The Rock House Method®**, the world's leading musical instruction system. Over his 20 plus year career, he has produced and/or appeared in more than 100 instructional products. Millions of people around the world have learned to play music using John's easy-to-follow, accelerated program.

John is a virtuoso guitarist who has worked with some of the industry's most legendary entertainers. He has the ability to break down, teach and communicate music in a manner that motivates and inspires others to achieve their dreams of playing an instrument.

As a guitarist and songwriter, John blends together a unique style of rock, metal, funk and blues in a collage of melodic compositions that are jam-packed with masterful guitar techniques. His sound has been described as a combination of vintage guitar rock with a progressive, gritty edge that is perfectly suited for today's audiences.

Throughout his career, John has recorded and performed with renowned musicians like Doug Wimbish (who's worked with Joe Satriani, Living Colour, The Rolling Stones, Madonna, Annie Lennox and many more top flight artists), Grammy Winner Leo Nocentelli, Rock & Roll Hall of Fame inductees Bernie Worrell and Jerome "Big Foot" Brailey, Freekbass, Gary Hoey, Bobby Kimball, David Ellefson (founding member of seven time Grammy nominee Megadeth), Will Calhoun (who's worked with B.B. King, Mick Jagger and Paul Simon), Jordan Giangreco from the acclaimed band The Breakfast, and solo artist Alex Bach. John has also shared the stage with Blue Oyster Cult, Randy Bachman, Marc Rizzo, Jerry Donahue, Bernard Fowler, Stevie Salas, Brian Tichy, Kansas, Al Dimeola and Dee Snyder.

For more information on John and his products visit RockHouseMethod.com.

MEMBER CODE

To download the lesson video and audio backing tracks that correspond with this book use the member number and register at RockHouseMethod.com

CODE
UK747858